THE
POCKET
GARDENER

THE POCKET GARDENER

Copyright © Summersdale Publishers Ltd, 2016

Illustrations © Shutterstock and Kostiantyn Fedorov

Summersdale Publishers Ltd
46 West Street
Chichester
West Sussex
PO19 1RP
UK

www.summersdale.com

Printed and bound in the Czech Republic

ISBN: 978-1-84953-802-2

Substantial discounts on bulk quantities of Summersdale books are available to corporations, professional associations and other organisations. For details contact Nicky Douglas by telephone: +44 (0) 1243 756902, fax: +44 (0) 1243 786300 or email: nicky@summersdale.com.

THE POCKET GARDENER

FELICITY HART

CONTENTS

INTRODUCTION

There is no better way to spend a day than pottering in the garden. Whether digging, planting, pruning or simply relaxing and enjoying the fruits of your labours, a garden can do wonders for your body, mind and soul. One of the trickiest parts of horticulture is keeping track of all the tasks required and that's where this little book comes in. *The Pocket Gardener* will guide you through the gardening year, season by season. From the first daffodils of spring to the last frosts of winter, each section contains helpful tips, reminders and 'how-to's, along with intriguing garden lore and inspiring quotes that will have you itching to pull on your wellies and head out the door. From choosing plants that will attract beneficial insects to making your own eco-friendly weed killer, this practical guide contains all the advice you need to make the most of your garden right through the year.

SPRING

Every spring is the only
spring, a perpetual
astonishment.

Ellis Peters

INTRODUCTION

One of the great joys of gardening is watching the garden come to life after winter. By mid-March the trees are starting to blossom and spring bulbs are beginning to peep above the ground. It's an exciting time of year to be a gardener; the air is full of potential and the warmer days herald the start of a range of gardening tasks. Now is the time to prepare beds, sow seeds, cut back shrubs and tidy up around the garden after its winter slumber. There's nothing more guaranteed to put a spring in your step than plunging your hands into the dirt again!

LAWN

At this time of year, the lawn is actively growing. If it's to stay in tip-top condition, it will need feeding, weeding and regular mowing.

SEEDING AND RE-TURFING

New lawns can be sown from late March onwards. Sowing a lawn gives you lots of options in terms of what grass you grow; however, it is by no means instant, and seeds are prone to being eaten by birds or washed away. An alternative option is to lay down turf. Turf comes ready-made, but it can be costly and it limits your choice of grass. The most important thing to remember, whichever option you choose, is to make sure you water the patch thoroughly for the first few weeks to allow for adequate germination and rooting.

MOWER MAINTENANCE

The mowing year begins in earnest in March, when mature grass begins to grow with vigour, and ends in October, when growth stops. (However, with recent changes in climate conditions, you can expect your lawn to be active well outside of this window!) Aim to mow the lawn once a week in spring and autumn, but you may need to mow twice a week in the height of summer. Mow only when the grass is dry – mowing wet grass can lead to roots being stripped out and moss growing in its place.

Repair damaged edges and bare patches using either fresh grass seed or new turf. Make sure the new seed or turf matches the original, otherwise you may end up with a patchwork-quilt effect!

GARDEN LORE

An old farmer's proverb tells us 'if you till the soil in April showers, you will have neither fruit nor flowers'.

TREES AND SHRUBS

BUDS GALORE

Flowering trees and shrubs are a sure sign that spring has arrived. They provide a guaranteed burst of colour in your garden each year, from the delicate pink and white blossoms of cherry trees to the spectacular blooms of azaleas and rhododendrons. Trees and shrubs use a lot of energy to produce flowers, leaves and seeds, so early March is a good time to begin feeding any established shrubs, trees and roses. You may opt to use a special rose or flowering shrub feed, or a general fertiliser, depending on the plant and the specific nutrients it requires. A plant will always tell you if it needs feeding. Telltale signs of struggle include a plant that is producing little new growth and leaves that are pale or yellowing.

PRUNING

Pruning in spring can encourage more flowering the following year. Early spring bloomers such as forsythia and Japanese quince can be pruned as soon as they have finished flowering. Check shrub roses for any signs of black spot disease and prune out any stems showing small purple-black spots. If this fungal infection is left to grow, the infected leaves will turn yellow and fall off. Try to pick off any early infections before they cause problems! Gather any infected leaves that have fallen and dispose of them – but remember not to add them to your compost pile, otherwise you risk spreading the fungus. This will significantly reduce the chance of another attack next year.

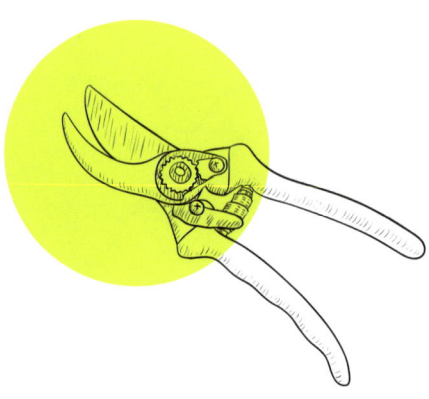

A garden without trees scarcely deserves to be called a garden.

Henry Ellacombe

FLOWERS AND HERBS

Spring bulbs bring a welcome splash of colour in the garden after the dark winter days. Everyone has their favourite flowers, but some varieties are universally popular.

FIRST FLOWERS

Daffodils are a delightful harbinger of spring – choose smaller varieties like narcissi to ensure they don't get blown over in bad weather. Snowdrops are another early spring bloomer. These tiny white flowers can often be seen poking up from beneath a layer of snow. Plant them in a partly shaded position in moist soil that drains well. Primroses grow best in partial shade and damp conditions. Crocuses like the shade, so should be planted around the base of a tree or hedge, whereas tulips are sun lovers, so put them in a sunny spot with good drainage.

If you're unsure about what flowers to introduce into a new garden, don't be afraid to seek advice from your local nursery. One way to ensure that a given plant is hardy enough for your garden is to look out for the Royal Horticultural Society Award of Garden Merit, which means the plant has been tested and approved by the RHS. And of course, it's better to use plants in your garden that are native to your area or that have been imported from areas with similar climates and soil.

GARDEN LORE

He who plants a garden plants happiness.

Earth laughs in flowers.

Ralph Waldo Emerson

GROW YOUR OWN HERBS

Many supermarkets stock ready-to-eat herb pots, which can be ideal for the kitchen. However, it's easy to treat them like any other consumable and forget to look after them. For a more lasting and eco-friendly option, plant herbs in your garden instead. Many small herb plants are available in garden centres and nurseries. Herbs such as rosemary and mint are ideal for a sunny garden as they are drought resistant and will thrive without any special attention; however, you may want to plant them in pots rather than sink them into the soil, to restrict their rampant growth.

FRUIT AND VEG

A TASTE OF THE GOOD LIFE

You needn't have an allotment to enjoy some home-grown produce. Plenty of veg can be grown in pots, such as bell peppers, chilli peppers, aubergines and tomatoes. Onions are a staple in countless dishes and, what's more, they are incredibly easy to grow – plant your baby onions (sets, as they are known) in spring, to harvest in late summer once the leaves have turned brown. If planting vegetables from seeds, as a general rule, the larger the vegetable seed, the deeper it should be sown. For carrots, you will need to sow half an inch below the surface; for beans, about 2 inches.

All kinds of salads can be grown indoors on a windowsill, away from the elements, meaning that

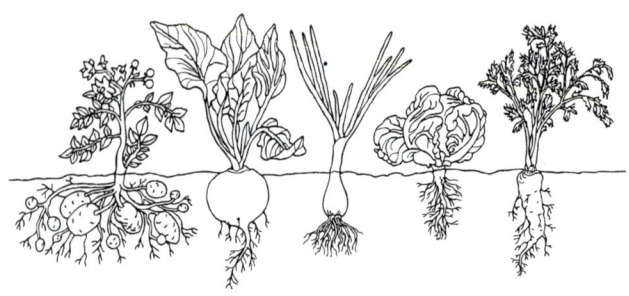

you're guaranteed a tasty treat without putting in lots of effort – and they'll keep growing back! A good tip to help your newly-planted seeds on their way is to place a layer of cling film over your tray or pot – this will help keep the moisture in while they germinate.

Once seedlings start to appear, remove the film. As soon as your salad leaves are around 3 inches tall you can start cutting.

FEELING FRUITY

Growing your own fruit can be very rewarding, not least because it is so versatile when it comes to turning it into pudding! If you're considering planting a fruiting tree, remember to take into consideration how much room it will need so that it has enough space to flourish. Establish whether or not it's self-fertilising or if it will need to be paired with another tree to encourage cross-pollination. Self-fertilising trees suited for the UK include Queen Cox apples and Brown Turkey figs. If trees sound heavy going, why not grow some berry plants? Strawberries can be grown in pots, borders or even hanging baskets.

STRAWBERRIES WITH LIME AND PEPPER SYRUP

This sweet, citrusy dessert is a new twist on strawberries with balsamic vinegar. It is best served with vanilla or coconut ice cream, or plain cream

Ingredients

2 limes
100 g golden caster sugar
2 tsp crushed black peppercorns
450 g ripe strawberries, hulled and cut into halves or quarters

Method

1. Use a vegetable peeler to pare the zest of 1 lime in long strips, and remove any white pith from the zest (this can make it taste bitter).

2. Squeeze both of the limes and add the juice to a medium pan, along with the zest, 3 tbsp of water, the sugar and the peppercorns.

3. Heat gently until the sugar has dissolved, stirring constantly, then bring to the boil and take off the heat.

4. Place the strawberries in a serving dish and pour over the hot syrup, making sure it coats all the strawberries.

5. Allow the syrup to cool (it will turn a rosy pink colour) and serve at room temperature with ice cream or cream.

BIRDS AND BEES

NESTING TIME

If you keep your eyes peeled throughout late March and April, you may see signs of birds building their nests. They only spend a small part of the year – often just a few days – building their new homes,  but if you are looking out of your window at the right time, you may see them collecting their building materials (typically grass, moss and small twigs).

SPRINGTIME PESTS

If you have a vegetable patch, planting coreopsis, feverfew and sweet alyssum in the vegetable bed will attract beneficial insects 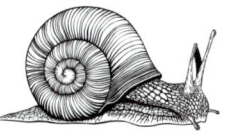 that will happily munch away on pests such as aphids and whiteflies. Lavender is not only sweet smelling but will also deter slugs, snails and aphids, and chives grown among rose bushes will help repel ants.

PONDS AND ROCKERIES

CREATING A HOME FOR NATURE

A pond is perhaps the most diverse way of introducing new creatures into your garden – it can create homes for a host of insects and amphibians, which in turn can help keep garden pests to a minimum. If you plan to keep fish, however, be aware that they may be inclined to eat any frog spawn that's in the pond. Birds, including ducks, may visit to bathe or drink. Ensure that your pond has shallow and deep areas, along with sloping sides to make it easier for creatures to climb in and out.

A pool is the eye of the garden in whose candid depths is mirrored its advancing grace.

Louise Bebe Wilder

BEDS AND BASKETS

SPRING BULBS

Keep spring-flowering bulbs in tip-top condition by feeding them with a general fertiliser. Spread the fertiliser around individual bulbs or larger clumps and rake the fertiliser in gently.

If the bulb is growing in a grassed area, omit the fertiliser and simply water in thoroughly.

As the weather starts to warm up, you can plant summer-flowering bulbs such as lilies, ornamental alliums, gladioli, *Camassia*, *Triteleia*, *Eucomis* and *Crocosmias*. These bulbs are perfect for beds and borders. Lilies and alliums also thrive in deep pots of well-drained compost and look stunning on a patio or terrace when they bloom in the summer.

HANGING BASKETS

Hanging baskets are a great way of adding colour and interest to a garden. Baskets are most often planted with vibrant bedding plants which flower during the summer, but they can also be planted with herbs, shrubs and evergreens for a long-lasting display.

Plant your baskets in early spring and keep them in a greenhouse or porch until late May or early June, after the risk of frost has passed (unless you've chosen frost-hardy flowers and tough evergreens, of course).

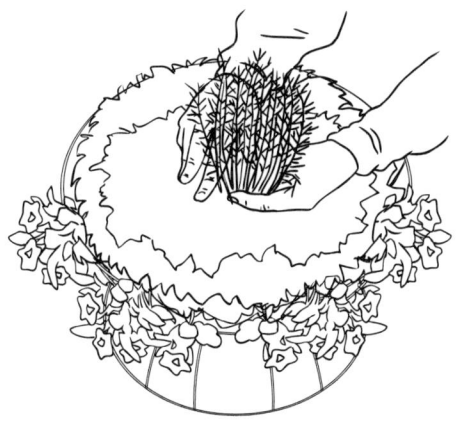

What to do:

- If you are using a standard wire basket, cover the inside of the basket with a 1.5 cm-thick layer of ready-made fibrous liner material (available in garden centres).

- If you are planting short-lived displays, half fill the basket with a multipurpose compost. If your display will last for more than one growing season, use a 'heavier' compost with long-lasting nutrients.

- Start by adding one central plant and then add some trailing plants around this, which will eventually cover the sides of the basket.

- Once all the plants are in, carefully add more compost, firming it gently around the plants.

- Push in some controlled-release fertiliser pellets or plugs and water well.

Aftercare:
- Hanging baskets can easily dry out so check them every day in the summer and water them regularly. Baskets tend not to dry out as much during the winter, but they still need to be checked. The compost needs to be kept moist but not soggy. Deadhead the flowers regularly to encourage more flower production and feed once a week with a liquid fertiliser from April to September.

TRUGS AND DIBBERS

DIG OUT YOUR DIBBER

Dibbers (or diggers) are one of the most ancient garden tools. They come into their own in spring as they make bulb and seed planting effortless. They were originally long sticks made from stone or animal bones, with a sharpened end which was used to dig a hole in the soil. Nowadays, most dibbers are made from wood, but an old screwdriver will work just as well. Using a dibber when planting seedlings is a great way to make sure the holes for your seedlings are all the same depth. Preparing holes in this way also ensures that your stem or root cuttings don't get damaged by being forced into the ground.

GARDEN LORE

One year's seeding is seven years' weeding.

SHEDS AND GREENHOUSES

IN PRAISE OF SHEDS

Many people would say that having a shed is one of the best things about a garden – a little bit of man-made order in among all that wildness. If you're lucky enough to have space for a shed and are buying one new, look to site it in a sheltered but accessible spot in the garden. It's not usually necessary to obtain planning permission to erect a shed, but it may be worth consulting your local council office just in case.

When storing tools, take a little time to keep them in good working order. Help prevent rust by wiping the metal portions of your tools down with an oily rag after each use, and be sure to hang tools up, away from the ground. Running a file over any cutting edges can help keep them sharp – just be sure to use protective eyewear and gloves.

GREENHOUSE GROWING

April is the time to plant out any young greenhouse tomatoes or pepper plants. You can transfer them into their final pots and place them in a conservatory or sunny porch, or plant them directly into the greenhouse border soil.

In May there's still time to sow late-summer vegetable seeds, such as French beans, runner beans, courgettes, marrows, sweetcorn, squash and pumpkins into individual pots or cells. Once you've sown your seeds, keep them in the greenhouse (or a warm windowsill) and take care not to overwater, the compost only needs to be just moist.

Later in May, once the frosts have passed, it should be safe to plant out summer beds. When planting out from your greenhouse the plants will need to be acclimatised to life in the garden for a few days. Place the plants in a sheltered position in front of a south-facing wall or hedge and cover with fleece to protect against sun scorch and temperature shock. They will appreciate the extra love and care!

Who loves a garden, loves
a greenhouse too.

William Cowper

SOIL

COMPOST

One of the simplest ways to improve your soil is to add organic matter in the form of compost. This will improve soil structure – helping sandy soil retain moisture and breaking down clumpy clay soil – as well as introducing microorganisms that create plant-available nutrients. The ideal compost heap will be no smaller than 1 m³; consist of around 50 per cent green material (grass trimmings, weeds, fruit and veg scraps, etc.) and 50 per cent brown woody material (wood chips, dead leaves, card, etc.); and be constructed in layers.

Things to leave out of your compost include: cooked food, meat scraps, droppings, perennial weed roots, diseased plant material, thick woody stems and prickly leaves.

SOIL CONDITION

A pH kit will help you decide what plants will suit your soil and whether or not to use a soil conditioner. An ideal pH level for most plants is between 6.0 and 7.5. You needn't stop at compost if you're keen to improve the condition of your soil. Here's a table showing a number of other popular conditioners and their effects:

Conditioner Effects
Composted bark (or mulch): improves aeration and drainage in clay soils.
Manure: enriches nutrients and encourages worms, giving better aeration.
Lime: neutralises acidity in sandy soils.

As well as conditioning your soil, it's best to select plants that will thrive in its existing state. Plants like heather, witch hazel, camellias and rhododendrons will fare well in acidic soils. For alkaline soils, things like lilac, Madonna lily, delphiniums, poppies and mock orange will do well.

SOIL TYPE

As well as assessing the pH level of your soil, it's useful to have an idea of its basic make-up. If you turn your soil and you find stones littered throughout, it's likely that you have chalky soil – this will be highly alkaline and will dry out quickly. Clay soil is easily identified by its dense consistency – it will need a lot of loosening for adequate aeration. Conversely, sandy soil, being fine, will lose moisture quickly and will be lacking in healthy organic matter.

Loam soil, with a mix of sand, silt and clay, is ideal.

Gardening is not a rational act. What matters is the immersion of the hands in the earth.

Margaret Atwood

POTTING

CHOOSING A POT

One main point to consider when buying pots, aside from the essential questions of drainage and adequate size, is how well the pot's material will suit the plant that's going to be living in it. Traditional terracotta pots are pleasing to the eye and a good choice for plants that rely on good drainage, as they are porous and will allow soil  to dry out quickly; however, they can sometimes crack after a heavy frost or snowfall. Heavier pots, made of wood, concrete or metal, are great for stabilising tall plants. Synthetic pots (plastic, etc.) are ideal for thirty plants, as they conserve moisture, and they can easily be slipped into a more decorative container.

LOCATION, LOCATION, LOCATION

Placing your potted plants in close proximity to one another will allow them to all benefit from the increased humidity this will create. For your indoor potted plants that rely on high humidity, such as orchids, bromeliads and other more exotic plants, try placing them together on a tray of damp gravel. However, be careful not to place pots so close that their leaves are obstructed, as this will restrict their growth.

DEADHEADING

Deadheading is essential for both indoor and outdoor potted plants. Pinch or cut off faded blooms to encourage further growth, making sure that the top part of the dead flower's stem comes off with it. This means the decaying stem won't affect any other healthy parts of the plant. If your plant has fine stems and very small flowers, it may benefit from an overall shearing, rather than a head-by-head tidy-up. Always dispose of deadheads, rather than leave them in the pot.

GARDEN LORE

A British tradition instructs that red and white flowers should not be given to someone in hospital, as these two colours together signify blood and bandages.

A good gardener always plants three seeds - one for the bugs, one for the weather and one for himself.

Leo Aikman

BINS AND BUTTS

BUY A BUTT

By late spring, conditions will be much drier and are likely to stay that way for several months. Now is the time to think about watering and water conservation. A water butt enables you to collect rainwater, which should provide all the water you need to keep your garden  alive as the weather hots up. Butts are easy to attach to your house and any other building that has a gutter and a downpipe, such as a shed, garage or other garden building. It is estimated that around 24,000 litres of water can be collected from the average house roof every year.

WEATHER DAMAGE

The warmer days of spring can lull you into a false sense of security. Don't forget that frosts can still occur at this time of year. It's a good idea to keep an eye on the weather forecast, as tender new growth is particularly vulnerable to frost damage. Symptoms can vary from plant to plant, but general signs to look out for are dark brown or black patches on leaves, bud and leaf drop, and dieback (the progressive death of twigs, branches, shoots, or roots, starting at the tips) of shoots or the whole plant. When you are confident that the last frost has occurred, prune out any damaged areas on plants.

WEEDING

WICKED WEEDS

Bindweed is deceptively pretty but bad news, as it will strangle plants and shrubs in borders. As an alternative to weedkiller, try training it to grow up a bamboo cane placed close to the weed in spring. Dandelions are deep-rooted perennial weeds, so be sure to dig down far enough when cutting them out.

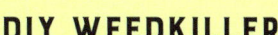

DIY WEEDKILLER

As a first step to tackling persistent weeds, you may want to try a home-made weedkiller.

Equipment

malt vinegar
water
spray bottle

Method

Mix two parts boiling water with one part malt vinegar and decant into a spray bottle; this method will also work with salt, though be sure you only use this if you're not going to attempt to grow anything else in the spot you're treating (the salt will sterilise the soil). Apply in dry, sunny conditions where possible.

CHEMICALS

If you feel you need to resort to a chemical weed killer, aim to use a selective agent over a non-selective one. If applying to your lawn, avoid cutting the grass for at least a week and don't put the treated cuttings in your compost pile. Always read up on the product you're considering using and follow the instructions of use carefully.

EDIBLE WEEDS

If your efforts to rid your garden of weeds are not paying off, then all is not lost – the right kind of weeds can be prepared for eating! Chickweed, clover, daisy flowers and leaves, and dandelions can all be mixed in with salads to add some new and interesting flavours. Nettles can be used as a substitute for spinach and, of course, to make a tasty, fresh soup.

Why not try making some dandelion-flower vinegar? Simply wash the flower heads off, add them to a sterilised jam jar full of cider vinegar and leave for around six weeks before using – delicious used in salad dressings!

Weeds are flowers too, once you get to know them.

A. A. Milne

NOTES

....
....
....
....
....
....
....
....
....
....
....
....
....
....
....
....
....
....
....
....

SPRING

....
....
....
....
....
....
....
....
....
....
....
....
....
....
....
....
....
....
....
....
....
....
....

....
....
....
....
....
....
....
....
....
....
....
....
....
....
....
....
....
....
....
....
....
....
....

SUMMER

I know that if odour were visible as colour is, I'd see the summer garden aureoled in rainbow clouds.

Robert Bridges, from *The Testament of Beauty*

INTRODUCTION

Summer is a busy time of year in the garden. By now, everything is planted and growing – so it's the ideal time to monitor your garden and catch any problems early on. Pesky weeds love the summer heat, so weeding will be top of your to-do list, along with watering, deadheading and mowing (nothing says summer like the sound of a buzzing lawnmower!). The warmer weather means you can enjoy being outdoors for longer. So in between gardening tasks, make sure you take the time to sit back, relax and enjoy the scents, sights and sounds of your garden.

LAWN

Proper maintenance is an essential part of lawn health.

MOWING FREQUENCY

As spring turns to summer, continue to mow your lawn regularly. How often you need to mow your lawn will depend on the conditions where you live and the local weather, but for most people, twice a week is about right. Remember to add small amounts of clippings to your compost heap. A special activator can also be used to convert clippings into useful compost.

BROWN PATCHES

Lawns will often turn brown during dry weather. If this happens, don't panic! Most turf grasses are amazingly resilient. Unless the lawn was recently sown or laid it will turn green again as soon as the weather gets wetter. Drop mowing to once a week during periods of drought. A good tip is to set the mower blades high so that the grass is left slightly longer, as this makes it more drought resistant.

WATERING

If your lawn was laid or sown earlier in the year or last autumn, it will benefit from an occasional thorough watering, especially during periods of very dry weather. Older, established lawns can generally be left to their own devices. Consider applying a summer lawn feed. It's important to apply the feed to grass that is not drought stressed and which has slightly moist soil beneath. If using a dry feed, make sure you water it in well to avoid any risk of scorching. Feeding and watering in the evening will help parched lawns absorb it more efficiently, as well as help conserve the water table.

MESSY MOSS

Towards the end of summer, as the weather gets damper, moss may rear its ugly head. For some this isn't a problem, but if you can't stand the sight of it, you can apply a moss killer to the lawn. Persistent moss growth is often a sign of poor growing conditions, such as acidic soil, a lack of feed, insufficient aeration or poor drainage. Killing and removing the moss is a good start, but to keep it at bay you may need to improve the overall health of the lawn and address any contributory factors.

Grass is the cheapest plant to install and the most expensive to maintain.

Pat Howell

There is always music amongst the trees in the garden, but our hearts must be very quiet to hear it.

Minnie Aumonier

TREES AND SHRUBS

SPLENDID SHRUBS

Cut back any flowering shrubs as soon as flowering is over to encourage a second flush of flowers later in the summer. Deadhead roses promptly to keep them blooming – it's a good idea to carry a sharp pair of secateurs around with you so you always have them to hand. Trim hedges regularly, too, to encourage more dense growth. At this time of year there are unlikely to be any nesting birds, but it's best to check!

GARDEN LORE

According to an ancient British tradition, the secret to eternal youth is to carry an acorn about your person, as oaks are known for living to a ripe old age.

FLOWERS AND HERBS

SUMMER FEED

Summer-flowering container plants need feeding regularly with a liquid tomato fertiliser in order to encourage the maximum number of flowers. If the compost is very dry, water lightly before applying the feed.

CHOOSE AUTUMN BULBS

As the summer progresses, autumn-flowering bulbs will start to become available in garden centres. *Colchicums*, *Nerines* and autumn crocuses are all good performers. Choose a sunny, well-drained spot to plant them in and they should last for years and years. You can also order autumn-flowering bulbs from specialist bulb catalogues and nurseries.

GIVE HERBS A HAIRCUT

If your herbs are in need of a trim, cut them back with scissors or shears. This will encourage new growth and will prevent them from becoming straggly. Keep chives trimmed to 6 or 7 inches high and be sure to pinch out the stems of any flowers. This will encourage new growth for the autumn and possibly early winter, too.

FRUIT AND VEGETABLES

By June, it should be warm enough to plant out any vegetables you have raised yourself from seed or bought from a garden centre, providing they have been hardened off properly. Hardening off is the process of introducing your seedlings, etc. to direct sunlight, dry air and cold temperatures bit by bit, for ever-increasing portions of the day, until they are happy to be outside full-time.

TOMATO TIPS

Tomatoes, peppers and aubergines will all need regular feeding during the summer. Use a high-potash liquid, such as tomato feed, and apply every week or two; this will encourage more flowers and good-sized fruits. Make sure you regularly remove the side shoots from tomato plants (the small nodes that will try to grow in the crook of branches); this will prevent the plant from becoming too bushy and it will focus the plant's energy on its existing trusses. If the plant becomes very leafy, remove some of the foliage so that light can ripen the fruit. Don't remove too many leaves – no more than one-fifth is about right – as the plant needs some leaves in order to be able to feed itself!

If a tomato plant shows splitting on the fruits, this could be a sign that the plant has not been watered consistently. Keep the soil moist at all times.

SALAD DAYS

Now is the time to sow your favourite salad crops. Crops such as lettuce, rocket, beetroot and radish can either be grown in containers or in open ground. Once you've sown the seeds, water them and cover with a mesh in order to keep birds and cats away.

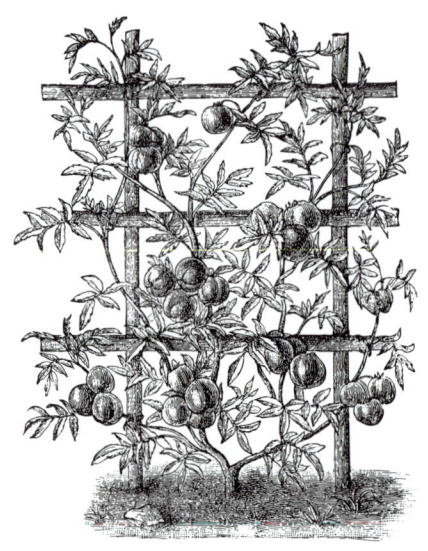

Gardeners, I think,
dream bigger dreams
than emperors.

Mary Cantwell

SUPER SPUDS

Choose a dry day to harvest your potatoes. When the soil is just starting to dry out, it won't cling as much to the tubers, which  makes life a lot easier! To check whether the potatoes are ready to be harvested, carefully scoop away the soil at the base of a plant and check the size of the tuber. If they are too small, replace the spoil and leave it a week or two before checking again. If the foliage is healthy, add it to the compost heap. If it is sickly or discoloured in any way, however, bin or burn it.

GARLIC AND ONION

It's pretty easy to tell when garlic and onion is ready to harvest. As soon as their foliage starts to yellow and flop, use a fork to gently ease the bulbs from the soil and leave them to dry off on the soil surface for a few days. If you're not eating your crop straight away, hang the bulbs up in a cool, well-ventilated place, away from any direct heat. If the stems are still bendy and you're feeling creative, you can plait the stems to make an attractive wall hanging!

ROASTED GARLIC AND BEAN DIP

This moreish dip is perfect for summer barbecues.
Serve it with vegetable crudités or pitta bread.

Ingredients

(makes one small bowl)
400 g can of cannellini beans, drained and rinsed
1–2 bulbs of garlic (depending on how garlicky you
like your dip!)
3 tbsp fresh dill (or parsley)
4 tbsp olive oil
Salt
Pepper

Method

1. Heat the oven to 180°C.

2. Cut ½ inch from the top of the garlic bulb to expose the cloves. Drizzle with olive oil, wrap in foil and bake for 50 to 60 minutes or until the garlic is soft. Allow to cool slightly, then squeeze each garlic clove from its skin.

3. Place all the ingredients, except the olive oil, into a food processor and blend until smooth. Add a large pinch of salt and a grinding of black pepper. Adjust to taste.

4. With the processor running, slowly pour in the olive oil (add more or less depending on the consistency you would like).

Serve in a bowl, garnished with fresh dill and a drizzle of olive oil.

SUMMER FRUITS

As soon as you've picked the last raspberries of the season, cut the canes that have borne fruit to within 5 cm of the ground.

As summer draws to a close, some early cropping apples may be ripening. To check whether the fruit is ready to harvest, cup an apple in your hand and give it a gentle twist. If the apple comes away easily in your hand it is ripe and ready to harvest.

The garden suggests
there might be a place
where we can meet
nature halfway.

Michael Pollan

BIRDS AND BEES

PEST PATROL

Take a few minutes to wander around your garden, checking for pests. This is an essential summer job which needs to be done on a regular basis. Don't just look at the leaves – turn them over and also peer into the depths of plants. Give your garden a thorough check-up!

If you discover an aphid infestation (see below), there's an eco-friendly solution. Buy a 'Grow Your Own Ladybird Kit', which will enable you to grow ladybirds from eggs before releasing them into the garden. If slugs are a problem, fill a plastic tub or cup with beer and leave it on top of the soil, next to the affected plant. Keep snails away from potted plants by smearing Vaseline around the edge of the pot every couple of weeks. If it's earwigs you need to get rid of, fill a flowerpot with crumpled-up tissue and place the pot upside down on a stick next to the infested plant. The earwigs will be tempted away from the plant into their new, cosy home.

CATERPILLARS

Caterpillars are a common garden pest. Signs to look out for include holes nibbled in leaves and tiny black-brown droppings, or 'frass'. You're most likely to spot the culprit at dusk when the caterpillars are feeding. You could consider treating the infestation with a biological control, which will kill off the caterpillars without harming other animals. A better solution is to stop adult butterflies and moths from laying their eggs in the first place. Edible crops can be covered with a fine mesh or fleece, which forms a barrier around the plant. Mesh and fleece tunnels are also effective.

An addiction to gardening is not all bad when you consider all the other choices in life.

Cora Lea Bell

ANT ATTACK!

Ants can be a menace for a number of reasons. Firstly, ant bites can be painful, especially if you experience lots in one go! But their tunnelling can also loosen soil around plant roots, resulting in the plant not being able to absorb water from the soil through its fine root hairs.

To exterminate ants, disturb their nests using a garden fork and then apply an ant killer. If you buy a biological ant killer, it will kill the ants without being a risk to wildlife or pets. If you keep hens, then you have an eco-friendly alternative. Simply disturb the ant nest and invite your hens over for an impromptu feast!

GARDEN LORE

In ancient Greece, farmers believed that the best way to rid their crops of a mouse infestation was to write them a letter suggesting they find somewhere else to live!

PONDS AND ROCKERIES

WATER LEVELS

Water levels in ponds can drop dramatically during the warmer months due to evaporation, so top up your pond or water feature occasionally. This will also introduce oxygen to your pond, making it a healthier environment for pond wildlife and plants.

POND LIFE

Consider adding some floating plants, such as water lilies, to your pond. These plants should establish themselves fairly quickly, adding beauty to your water feature. By lying flat on the pond's surface, water lilies create shade, which dramatically reduces the growth of pond pests such as algae blanket weed and the dreaded 'pea soup' pond!

PEA SOUP

If your pond turns an alarming shade of bright green, this will be due to a massive growth of algae in the water. It's tempting to change the water, but if you add fresh hose water to a pond it will take a while to rebalance itself. Instead, add more oxygenator plants and plants which float on the surface, such as water lilies. Barley straw can also help to banish algae. The easiest way to use it is to stuff some old tights with bundles of barley straw (from garden centres) and add this to the pond, weighing it down with a large stone or brick. You can also buy barley straw pads, which can be dropped into your pond.

GARDEN LORE

An old wives' tale believes that you will have good luck all year if the first butterfly you see is white.

BEDS AND BASKETS

MORE DEADHEADING!

It may seem like a thankless task, but regular deadheading is worth the hassle. If left to form seed heads, the plant's energy will be diverted away from the business of producing more flowers. Regularly deadheading herbaceous perennials and summer bedding plants encourages more flowers and prolongs the flowering period.

CARING FOR CONTAINERS

Plants in pots or containers will need regular watering throughout the summer. Ensure that the water penetrates right down to the base of the container and water twice a day if necessary! Grouping containers together can help as they will provide some shade for each other. However, some plants may benefit from being moved to a cooler position, out of direct sunlight. Hanging baskets can also be taken down and moved to a more shaded spot, especially if you are away for more than a day. In addition to regular watering, feed summer-flowering container plants with a liquid tomato fertiliser to encourage flowering.

Flowers are beautiful hieroglyphics of nature, with which she indicates how much she loves us.

Johann Wolfgang von Goethe

TRUGS AND DIBBERS

BUYING TOOLS

Before going out and buying every shiny new tool you see, take some time to consider what, realistically, you will need for the job at hand.
Seek out places where you might find pre-owned tools – car boot sales, agricultural fairs and online auction sites. If you're buying new, talk to someone at your local garden centre to get an idea of reliable manufacturers and be sure to handle each tool before you buy it – there's no point in spending money on something that's uncomfortable to use!

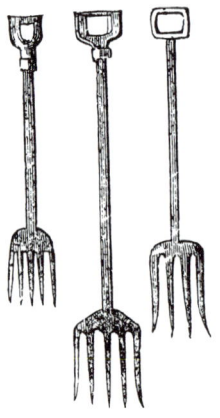

Once you've parted with your hard-earned cash for some quality tools, it is advisable to take a little time to keep them in good working order. (See p.31 for tips on how to look after tools.)

TRUG HISTORY AND MAINTENANCE

Trugs are traditional wooden baskets which are used for a variety of garden tasks – from harvesting vegetables and gathering cut flowers, to carrying kindling, logs and gardening tools. Their name is derived from the Anglo-Saxon 'trog', which means 'boat-shaped vessel'. Trug-making goes back to the sixteenth century, when they were used as measures or scoops for grain. The trug became famous when it was shown at the Great Exhibition in 1851 and Queen Victoria ordered several for members of the royal family.

Wooden trugs are renowned for their strength and durability. They will last for years if they are well maintained. To keep your trug in good condition, avoid leaving anything damp in it and give it a lick of linseed oil once in a while.

Other people's tools
only work in other
people's gardens.

Arthur Bloch

SHEDS AND GREENHOUSES

Keep a close eye on plants that are kept in a greenhouse or under frames. In the summer months the temperature inside a greenhouse can become dangerously high, increasing the risk of scorching foliage and flowers. Keep the greenhouse vents and windows open as much as possible and consider applying a shading paint, or installing blinds on greenhouses to protect the plants inside.

BINS AND BUTTS

SUMMER COMPOSTING

Summer is a great time for composting. As temperatures rise and rain is less frequent, compost will boost the soil with added nutrients. In summertime, the compost pile is at peak decomposition and a hot summer sun can really help your pile to 'cook'. Keep an eye on your compost pile or bin and make sure it doesn't dry out. If it does, your compost pile will start to slow down. Aim to keep your pile or bin a little moist during dry spells and turn it using a spading fork to encourage air circulation. With enough organic waste, you should be able to produce several batches of compost throughout the summer. Don't forget to put your grass clippings in the compost bin after you've mown the lawn!

WATER ON TAP

A water butt will come into its own during the hot, summer months. Rainwater is better for plants than tap water for a number of reasons. Unlike tap water, it will be warmer than mains water so it will be less of a shock to the roots of a plant. Rainwater also contains no chlorine or other water treatments, which can damage plants. The exception to this general rule is young seedlings: water stored in a water butt can sometimes develop fungal spores which can be harmful to new seedlings, so these should be watered with tap water.

GARDEN FURNITURE

You may think choosing garden furniture is simply a matter of taste, but in fact it pays to think about things like colour in terms of how your furniture will blend with the overall look of your garden – darker shades of paint or plain wood will not detract your eye from the flowers and plants you have in your garden. Space is another key issue: think about purchasing furniture which will give you storage options – e.g., a hinged lid seat.

It's a good idea to regularly hose off garden furniture – especially tables – in order to remove any food or drink spillages. This should mean fewer wasps inviting themselves to your barbecue or picnic!

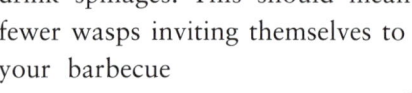

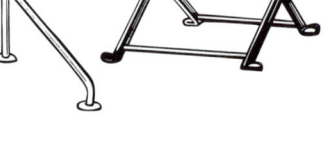

Do not spread the compost on the weeds.

William Shakespeare

HOW TO WATER

It goes without saying that regular watering is essential during the summer months – for bedding plants, vegetables, pots and hanging baskets, as well as newly planted trees and shrubs. The following tips will help you water your way to happy plants:

- Always water your plants in the cool of the evening or very early morning. If you water your plants during the heat of the day, there's a good chance a lot of it will evaporate before it reaches the plant roots.

- The part of the plant that needs water is the roots, so water the soil, not the leaves.

- In hot weather, give each plant a good soaking every 2–3 days, rather than a quick watering every day.

- If you have to prioritise, water plants that need it the most (i.e., pots, hanging baskets, shallow-rooted plants – such as bedding and young vegetables – and new plants that don't yet have a well-established root system).

- Help feed water to the roots of thirsty plants by sinking a flower pot into the soil alongside the plant. This will channel water down into the soil.

- Choose large containers for your plants as these won't dry out as quickly as small ones. Add water-retaining granules to the compost in pots and hanging baskets.

- To save money, use rainwater collected in a water butt. You can also use waste water from washing up and the water from baths and showers. Avoid using water that contains bleach or strong household cleaning products, as this could damage the plants.

THE ART OF WEEDING

Weeds grow phenomenally fast at this time of year so it's imperative to keep on top of this garden chore. This isn't purely for aesthetic reasons; weeds will compete with flowers and vegetables for water and nutrients, and if they are allowed to go to seed, they will produce hundreds more weeds! Once established, they can be hard to remove without damaging surrounding plants. By weeding all areas of your garden as often as you can you will be saving yourself time in the long run.

Weeding tips:

- Weed your garden at least once a week. Young weeds will not have a mature root system, so will be easier to pull up.

- The best time to weed a garden is after it has rained (or after watering). When the ground is wet, the roots of the weeds will come out of the ground more easily.

- Pinch the weed as far down as possible, at the base of the stem, and gently but firmly pull the weed out of the ground. This pinch-and-pull method will ensure that some (if not all) of the roots will come away with the weed plant. Use a trowel or pointed implement to loosen the soil around the weed if necessary.

- Remove annual weeds with a hoe or special weeding tool. By severing the tops from the roots, the weed will not be able to produce seed and spread.

- Make sure you collect up all the weeds and dispose of them so that their seeds do not have a chance to go back into your lawn or garden – and remember not to compost them. (If you hoe off annual weeds during the heat of the day, simply leave the weeds on the surface of the soil, where they will wither and die.)

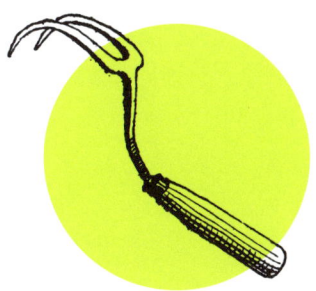

Look deep into nature, and then you will understand everything better.

Albert Einstein

NOTES

....
....
....
....
....
....
....
....
....
....
....
....
....
....
....
....
....
....
....
....
....
....
....
....

....
....
....
....
....
....
....
....
....
....
....
....
....
....
....
....
....
....
....
....
....
....
....
....
....
....

AUTUMN

Delicious autumn! My very
soul is wedded to it, and
if I were a bird I would fly
about the earth seeking the
successive autumns.

George Eliot

INTRODUCTION

Summer may be over but there's still plenty to do in the garden in autumn. As leaves burst into glorious colour, the garden will need clearing and preparing for the cold winter months ahead. Essential tasks include feeding the lawn, clearing the pond and, of course, raking up fallen leaves. It may be the end of the growing season but autumn is a great time to plant shrubs, prune fruit trees, and sow winter veg. Pull on your wellies and make the most of the dappled sunlight – it's a beautiful time of year to be out in the garden!

LAWN

Autumn is a good time to carry out lawn maintenance. However, if there has been heavy rain and the lawn is excessively wet wait for it to dry out a little before following any of the steps below, otherwise you risk damaging your lawn.

PREPARING LAWNS FOR WINTER

First, tackle any moss. Spread a moss killer across the lawn, and then wait the specified time on the packet before scarifying, or vigorously raking the lawn.

Use a spring-tined rake to scarify, to remove the moss and other debris. This will form a layer known as thatch, which can go on your compost heap.

Next, improve the drainage of your lawn by driving a garden fork into the ground as far as you can. Wiggle it backwards and forwards to make air channels and repeat this roughly every 10 cm, especially across areas of lawn that get heavy usage. These areas can become compacted which can cause problems with drainage, weeds and moss. For larger lawns, you can hire a powered aerating machine. The average lawn should only need aerating every two to three years.

Buy a ready-mixed bag of sandy top dressing from a garden centre and spread this across the surface of the lawn, so that it fills the holes but allows water and air to enter.

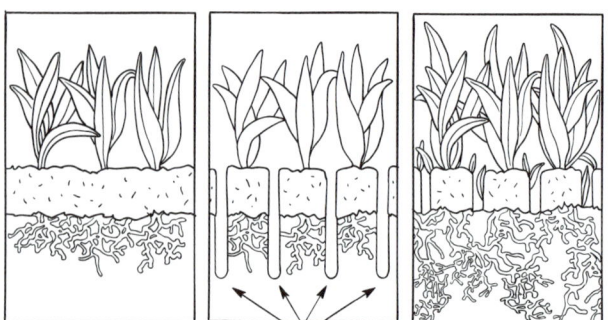

Finally, apply an autumn lawn fertiliser, which will perk up your lawn and help strengthen the grass, ready for the winter ahead.

Autumn is a good time to create a new lawn from seed or laid turf. You can also use a grass seed mixture to overseed any areas of existing lawn that have become patchy or bare.

FALLEN LEAVES

It's important to rake any fallen leaves from the lawn and from nets on ponds. Try to do this regularly so that the rain doesn't have a chance to turn the leaves into a solid, immovable mass! A thick layer of leaves will smother a lawn and weaken the grass, not to mention provide an ideal home for garden pests. Add any leaves you rake to your compost, layered with other bits of garden debris, and remember to keep some aside so that you can continue to build your compost over the winter months.

You can also turn the leaves you collect into leaf mould, which makes great mulch. Simply cram the leaves into black bin liners and add a litre or two of water. Tie the top of the liner or fold the top of the bag over and secure it with a brick. Punch a few rows of holes in the bag with a fork and store in a shady spot. By the following autumn, the bags will be full of a lovely, crumbly mixture that can be spread around the base of plants to provide insulation and nourishment over the winter months.

TOADSTOOL TROUBLE

Autumn is toadstool season! If several appear on your lawn, try brushing them off with a broom. If you do this before the caps have had a chance to open and spread their spores, this may well rectify the problem. However, if the toadstools keep returning, more drastic action may be required. The toadstools may be feeding off dead tree roots beneath the lawn. (Toadstools growing in lines can usually be found to be following the length of the root). If this is the case, you will need to cut away the turf and excavate the dead roots. Once you've done this, fill the gap with topsoil, firm well and replace the turf. With any luck, that will be the last you see of the toadstools!

TREES AND SHRUBS

The ideal time to plant out shrubs and trees is in the autumn, when the mix of sun and rain provide the ideal conditions for roots to establish themselves before the winter.

CHOOSE A TREE

Before going out and buying trees for your garden, be sure to look into their growth rate. Leave enough space between each tree (and any other potential obstacle, natural or otherwise) to ensure that there's enough water and sunlight to go around. Also, be aware that some trees will develop extensive, fast-growing root systems (poplar and willow are two examples) which may lead to subsidence if planted near to houses – take this into account, especially if your garden is in close proximity to your neighbour's.

[Autumn is] a second
spring when every leaf
is a flower.

Albert Camus

GARDEN LORE

Some Irish literature tells of a drink called 'hazelmead', a brew made from the nuts of hazel trees, which was supposed to be psychotropic, imparting visions and sacred wisdom.

TOLERANT TREES

If you live close to a road or in a more urban area where your trees are likely to encounter a considerable amount of air pollution, consider planting more tolerant trees. These could include:

- maple

- horse chestnut

- alder

- silver birch

- poplar

CREATIVE TOPIARY

Topiary is a great way to add a creative touch to your garden. If you fancy giving it a try, all you need is a chicken-wire frame, which should be available ready-made at your local garden centre, and a bit of patience. Once you've decided on a shape, pick a shrub that's roughly the same size (or slightly larger) – box or yew are good varieties for small topiaries – and fit your frame over it and pull the branches through the holes to encourage them to take the shape of the wire. As the shrub slowly grows, simply prune back and trim to create your leafy work of art.

I frequently tramped
eight or ten miles through
the deepest snow to keep
an appointment with
a beech tree, or a
yellow birch...

Henry David Thoreau

FLOWERS AND HERBS

If bad weather stops you from getting out in the garden, grab a mug of tea, put your feet up and have a look through some seed, young plant and bulb catalogues to see which flowers you would like to grow next year. It's easy to get carried away when choosing from catalogues, so take your time and choose selectively, to make sure you get what you need (and can afford!).

PLANT SPRING-FLOWERING BULBS

In early September you can begin to plant spring-flowering bulbs such as daffodils, crocus, tulips, snowdrops and miniature irises. They can go in beds, borders, pots and containers, and they can also be planted in the grass beneath trees and shrubs. If you have the space, you might like to plant a few bulbs specifically for cutting for the house. Make sure you follow any instructions included and plant the bulbs as deep as the pack suggests. It may take a little more effort but the bulbs should do better and you will be less likely to dig them up by mistake when you are planting other flowers nearby. Now is also the time to sow hardy annual flowers which will be ready to bloom next summer – nigella, cornflowers, Shirley poppies, larkspur, and so on.

DIVIDE AND CONQUER

Lift and divide clumps of herbaceous perennials, such as *Agapanthus* (lily of the Nile), that have become overcrowded. Replant the outer sections of the clump. You can discard the central parts as these parts will be weaker.

TIPS FOR SUCCESSFUL PLANTING

- Choose good, healthy plants which suit the soil type, as well as the size and aspect of the site.

- Prepare the site by removing any debris and weeds, and digging over the soil.

- Dig a good-sized hole to the depth suggested on the plant label and fork in some planting compost and fertiliser.

- If the plant's root ball is dry, let it soak in a bucket of water for a couple of hours before planting.

- Gently tease out the root ball to encourage the roots to grow out into the soil.

- Plant at the correct depth and firm the soil in well to prevent air pockets.

- Ensure the plant is kept well-watered.

PROLONGING HERBS

To protect potted herbs against the cold, either dig a hole and plunge the pots into the soil in a sheltered spot or insulate the pots to protect the roots. If leaving pots above ground, it's a good idea to raise them off the surface using special 'pot feet' (available from garden centres and pot suppliers). This will help with drainage and will reduce the risk of the plant becoming fatally waterlogged.

Herbs such as basil are too tender to be outside at this time of year, so try sowing a pot of basil seed to grow indoors. Place your pot on a warm windowsill and aim to keep the compost just moist at all times. You can also dig up a section of an established parsley or mint plant. Transfer this segment to a good-sized container with some fresh compost and place it on a well-lit windowsill. This should provide you with fresh herbs for the next few months.

FRUIT AND VEGETABLES

Don't neglect your veg plot! Plenty of vegetables can be grown throughout the coldest months. Cover young plants with netting to keep hungry birds out, and keep them well-watered and well-weeded to encourage them to establish themselves before winter arrives. If a hard frost is predicted, cover the plants with fleece to give them extra protection.

VEGETABLE TASKS

Onions and garlic are hardy plants which cope well with the cold winter weather. They are incredibly easy to grow and there should be a good selection of varieties to choose from for autumn planting. Bear in mind that onions and garlic have a long growing season so any that are planted out in the autumn won't be ready for harvesting until next summer. Rocket, spinach and pak choi can also be sown now.

In September, lift any potatoes that are still in the ground and leave them on the surface for a few hours to dry off. Put the tubers in a paper or hessian sack and store them in a dark, cool, frost-free place (e.g.

shed or garage). Don't store any tubers which look damaged or show any signs of pest attack – one rotting tuber will soon infect your whole bag of potatoes!

Tomato plants will deteriorate rapidly from now on, so pick any unripe tomatoes and place them in a paper bag with an overripe banana to encourage them to ripen. Once harvested, tomato, sweet chilli pepper and aubergine plants can safely be added to the compost bin or heap, providing they look healthy.

PRUNING FRUIT

Autumn is the start of the fruit-tree pruning season. Apple and pear trees can be pruned as soon as the trees are dormant. Each tree will require a different pruning method, so it's worth consulting a specialist fruit book to learn the right technique. Strawberry plants also need a good tidy-up at this time of year. Remove any discoloured leaves and runners from the plant, to ensure the plant puts its energy into producing the very best crop. Prune redcurrant, gooseberry and blackcurrant bushes to keep the centre of the bush open and spacious. This will allow air and sunshine to reach the stems, encouraging healthy fruit with little or no disease. Continue to pick apples and pears and either eat straight away or store them somewhere cool, such as a dark cellar, attic or garage.

APPLE, PEAR AND WALNUT CRUMBLE

Everyone loves a crumble! This traditional pudding will make the most of your apples and pears in autumn.

Ingredients
500 g apples, peeled, cored and cut into large chunks
500 g pears, peeled, cored and cut into large chunks

Zest of 1 lemon, finely grated
Juice of ½ lemon
2 tbsp light muscovado sugar

Crumble topping:

100 g walnuts
175 g wholemeal flour (or plain white)
85 g butter, diced
85 g caster sugar (or light muscovado sugar)

Method

1. Heat the oven to 190°C (fan 170°C/gas 5).

2. Put the apples, lemon zest, lemon juice and sugar in a saucepan and cook for 3–4 minutes.

3. Add the pears and cook for another 2–3 minutes, until the fruit is just beginning to soften.

4. Spoon the fruits and juices into a 1.7 litre pudding dish and spread evenly.Prepare the crumble by whizzing half the walnuts in a food processor until they resemble the consistency of ground almonds. Add the flour, butter and sugar and blitz to a coarse or fine crumble mixture, depending on your preference.

5. Break the remaining walnuts with your fingers and mix into the crumble.

6. Spoon the crumble mix on top of the fruits and bake for 20–25 minutes until golden.

7. Serve with custard or cream.

BIRDS AND BEES

Even in the autumn, there will be some pests eager to get into your garden. Now is the time that moles prepare for winter by fortifying their home and collecting food supplies. So you may see increased mole activity at this time of year. If you're plagued by a meddlesome mole, try sticking empty bottles upright, with their caps removed, in some of its hills (see right) – the sound of the wind blowing over the tops will help scare it away.

Cats can be distracted from getting in among your delicate flowers with a clump of strategically placed cat mint, while regular mint, spread around the borders of your garden, will deter mice – that is, if the cat doesn't get to them first!

If rabbits are a problem in your area, you may want to invest in some rabbit guards, which you can fit around the base of trees and shrubs. Rabbits can seriously damage plants by stripping bark with their sharp teeth.

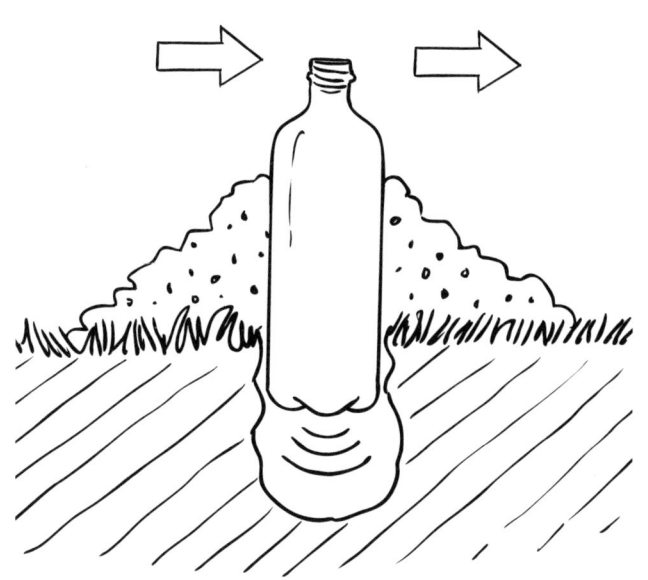

No occupation is so delightful to me as the culture of the earth, and no culture comparable to that of the garden.

Thomas Jefferson

PONDS AND ROCKERIES

ROCKERY IDEAS

Autumn is a good time to build a rock garden. There is less to do in the garden at this time of year, so you can take your time transforming a corner of your outside space into a striking feature which will be ready to plant in spring. Rock gardens are a great way to display alpines and other small plants, but many people make the mistake of thinking that alpines only flower in spring and summer. In fact, many flower from February to the end of October. And if you choose alpines with evergreen foliage, your rock garden will look fantastic year round.

Suitable autumn-flowering evergreen plants:

- *Gentiana sino-ornata* (showy Chinese gentian)

- *Crocus kotschyanus* (Kotschy's crocus)

- *Cyclamen hederifolium* (ivy-leaved cyclamen)

- *Sternbergia lutea* (winter daffodil)

- *Zephyranthes candida* (Peruvian swamp lily)

POND CLEARING

The best time to clean ponds is in late autumn as this is when many of their creatures are less active. Small ponds will need a thorough clean every five years, whereas large ponds need a complete overhaul every 10 years. Carefully cut back or lift out any over-vigorous plants and remove any debris. Take this opportunity to remove any electrical pumps from ponds and water features and store them for the winter. Electrical water pumps can be damaged by very cold weather. They can also get clogged up with dead algae and water debris. Dry them thoroughly before storing and lightly grease any metal parts if necessary, to keep them functioning smoothly. Finally, it's good idea to fit a net over ponds to catch any autumn leaves. If left to rot in the water, leaves produce gases which are toxic to fish.

WEATHER DAMAGE

GARDEN FURNITURE

If you won't be using items of garden furniture from now on, making this a good time to clean them and put them under cover so that they are protected from the harsh winter weather. Plastic furniture can be cleaned with soap and water and stored in a garage or garden shed. Don't be tempted to leave plastic furniture out over winter as even faint winter sunlight will deteriorate the compounds in plastic materials, which can become brittle over time. Hardwood furniture (made from durable wood such as teak, iroko and eucalyptus) can be left out over winter. Simply wash the furniture with a brush and soapy

water once a year to remove any algae and lichens. Metal garden furniture will need to be cleaned and checked for rust. Treat with rust-preventing paint if necessary before the wet weather sets in.

FENCE AND PLANT SUPPORT

Check arches, trellis and fencing to make sure they are in good order and secure enough to survive winter gales. Similarly, check to see if any plants require extra support. If the weather is unseasonably warm, autumn-flowering perennials – such as Japanese anemones, asters, and Michaelmas daisies – may grow larger than usual and might need some help to withstand heavy wind and rain. Trained fruit trees may also require attention. Make sure they are well secured to their posts and are able to bear a good buffeting by the wind.

Compared to gardeners,
I think it is generally
agreed that others
understand very little
about anything
of consequence.

Henry Mitchell

BINS AND BUTTS

RECYCLING WATER

As rainfall increases and the growing season comes to an end, there are plenty of ways to use up excess rainwater that has collected in your water butt. It's ideal for cleaning the car or for scrubbing the greenhouse, garden furniture and paving slabs. You can also use it to water house plants. If you haven't already, take the time to make sure your water butt has a filter fitted to keep out autumn leaves and moss, otherwise the water may quickly become a stagnant sludge! If you use up the water in your water butt, use water which has been used for baths and showers (known as 'grey water') to water the garden if it needs it. (Don't use it to water anything edible such as fruit and vegetables.)

GARDEN LORE

Be sure not to pick blackberries after St Michaelmas Day (11 October) as legend has it that the Devil marks them and makes them poisonous after this date.

COMPOSTING AUTUMN LEAVES

Autumn is a great time to start composting. As you tidy up your garden after the growing season, pick up fallen leaves to use in your compost pile. When adding them to your pile, alternate layers of leaves with other organic material (e.g. spent flowers, tomato plants, grass clippings and other garden debris) to prevent the leaves from matting and forming an impenetrable barrier to air and water. During rainy spells, cover the pile with a tarpaulin to prevent the compost from becoming waterlogged. And don't forget to turn your compost regularly to aerate it – this supplies the bacteria with oxygen and speeds up decomposition.

DEADLY DISEASES

Autumn is the time of year when you are most likely to see signs of fungal diseases, such as honey fungus and coral spot, on trees and shrubs.

HONEY FUNGUS

Honey fungus is one of the most feared diseases in the garden. Aggressive forms of this parasitic fungus can be lethal to trees and shrubs. Look out for honey-coloured mushroom-shaped toadstools, often growing in clumps around plants that look sickly. It's not the toadstools that do the damage, however, it's the white fungus material (mycelium) which lies beneath the bark or stem of the infected plant that can kill it within just a few months. Any infected trees or shrubs should be dug up as soon as possible, along with their entire root system. If you spot any blackish threads, which look a bit like bootlaces, protruding from the roots, remove these as well, as these are how the infection spreads beneath the soil.

CORAL SPOT

Coral spot is easy to see at this time of year as deciduous trees and shrubs lose their leaves, leaving a clear view of branches and stems. Look out for coral-pink raised spots or pustules, especially on *Acer* species (maples), *Elaeagnus*, figs and magnolias. This fungus can cause dieback, so cut or saw off any infected stems and bin or burn the infected material. The spores of this fungus spread by colonising dead branch stubs, so as a preventative measure, remove dead stems from trees and shrubs before you see any signs of an infection.

GARDEN LORE

Be sure to keep boundary fences in good order or you will invite quarrels with your neighbours.

A flower is an educated weed.

Luther Burbank

NOTES

....
....
....
....
....
....
....
....
....
....
....
....
....
....
....
....
....
....
....
....
....

....
....
....
....
....
....
....
....
....
....
....
....
....
....
....
....
....
....
....
....
....
....
....
....
....

WINTER

All gardeners need to know when to accept something wonderful and unexpected.

Allen Lacy

INTRODUCTION

Winter is the ideal time to take stock of your garden and plan for the year ahead. Do you need to change the size or shape of your lawn, flower beds or vegetable patch? Is it time to repave the patio or install that pergola you've been dreaming about? A crisp and cold winter's day is the perfect opportunity to tidy the garden, sort out the shed, and clean and repair tools. And there are still plenty of gardening tasks to get your teeth into, such as planting fruit trees and harvesting winter vegetables for hearty soups and stews!

LAWN

In winter, grass becomes dormant and virtually stops growing. However, you still need to care for your lawn to help it withstand the harsh winter weather and emerge in the best possible condition next spring.

KEEP OFF THE GRASS!

Avoid walking on lawns or other grassed areas when they are covered in frost or snow as this can damage the blades of grass (this is why you often see dead grass along countryside footpaths come springtime). You may discover, as the snow melts, that there are footprints etched into your lawn! Don't worry about removing snow from lawns, but note that if you build a snowman, the ground underneath it will probably take a long time to defrost. Once you've finished admiring your snowman, distribute the snow back over the lawn so it doesn't mark the grass.

KEEP RAKING

Regularly rake the lawn to keep it free of leaves. If leaves are left to build up, they can suffocate the grass and encourage fungal diseases. If you have a large area of lawn, consider using a lawnmower fitted with a collection bag or vacuum system.

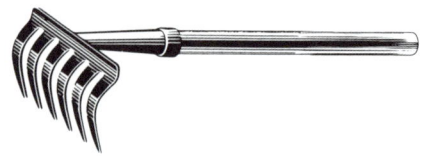

WINTER MOWING

It's a common belief that you can stop mowing a lawn in winter. However, providing the ground is not frozen, it's advisable to get the mower out and 'top' the grass. Set the blades so that you remove anything from 10 per cent to 25 per cent off the top of the grass. This will tidy it up and stimulate healthy growth.

GARDEN LORE

Robins are considered lucky. Wish upon the first robin you see in winter, and your wish will come true – but only if the robin remains in sight until you have finished saying your wish.

TREES AND SHRUBS

It's tempting to think that trees and shrubs are as tough as old boots, but they still need some TLC if they are to survive and thrive over winter.

NEWLY PLANTED TREES AND SHRUBS

Bare-root trees or shrubs that are planted in the autumn or over winter won't have had a chance to anchor themselves in the ground. This means the wind can easily rock them back and forth, resulting in them becoming loose. Check any plants that have recently been planted and firm them back in place if necessary. You may need

to stake any tall or exposed plants that are particularly vulnerable to the wind.

ESTABLISHED TREES AND SHRUBS

Once plants are established there is less risk of 'wind rock', but it's still advisable to check ties and stakes to ensure the plants are safely anchored. As a general rule, stakes should only be used for about 18 months. They are intended as a short-term support to help the tree establish in the soil. After this, if the tree is not firmly anchored, it suggests there may be something amiss with the tree or the way it was planted. Check that ties are the appropriate fit. If a tie is too loose, bark can become damaged as it rubs against it. On the other hand, if a tie is too tight, it can bite into a trunk as it expands and inhibit growth.

SNOW AND ICE

Snow settling on top of branches and shrubs is a beautiful sight, but sadly if the snow settles heavily it can cause a lot of damage. Gently shake the snow off or tap the branch with a cane to dislodge the extra weight. Severe frosts can also be a problem for tender buds on flowering shrubs such as magnolias. Keep them warm and snug by wrapping their top growth in some horticultural fleece.

If a tree is treated as a living organism, with an understanding of its vital functions, it will be a constant source of profit and pleasure to men.

N. T. Mirov

FLOWERS AND HERBS

Winter is a great time to prepare the soil in your flower beds and vegetable patches for planting over the coming months. Providing the soil is not too wet, you can dig or fork over areas to improve aeration and drainage, and incorporate garden compost or well-rotted manure to improve the soil condition if necessary.

TIME FOR TULIPS

If you haven't already planted your tulips, you should find them at rock-bottom prices in garden centres in early December. Provided the soil is not very wet or cold, you can plant tulips and daffodils now – they will just flower a few weeks later than everyone else's!

Now's the time to think ahead to summer bedding plants, such as lilies, alliums and dahlias. Garden centres and catalogues should give you plenty of

inspiration. As long as the soil is not too wet or frozen, these bulbs can be planted between now and March, depending on the flower you've chosen.

WATCH YOUR STEP!

Avoid the temptation to clear snow from your flower beds. Tender plants can benefit from a layer of snowfall – the snow acts like a blanket, insulating the plants from the cold weather to come. Avoid stepping on flower beds after heavy rain or snow, however. Wet soil is easily compacted by footsteps and this hinders drainage. If you need to stand on the soil, try laying boards over the surface to form a pathway, to spread the weight.

HARDY HERBS

Many herbs will continue to thrive over winter. Rosemary, mint, parsley, sage and thyme are all cold-hardy and should survive without any extra protection. Parsley in particular will keep growing, even through a layer of snow! Growth will slow down, however, so if you're a keen cook and use a lot of herbs, it's worth placing them in a cold frame to encourage growth. Even so, don't crop too much of the plant – it needs some left to keep itself alive!

When the world wearies, and society ceases to satisfy, there is always the garden.

Minnie Aumonier

FRUIT AND VEGETABLES

Even in the depths of winter, there's no reason for your veg plot to be bare. Despite the shorter daylight hours, some vegetables are actually best started at this time of year and crops such as Brussels sprouts, cabbages and leeks should be ready for harvesting.

PURCHASE A PROPAGATOR

Garlic, onions and shallots are happy to be planted now. You can also sow broad beans, winter lettuce and peas. If you haven't already got a heated propagator, consider treating yourself to one, as it will drastically increase the range of plants you can grow at this time of year. A heated propagator will keep your seeds at a constant temperature during the colder months and will provide the perfect warm, damp atmosphere for your seeds and cuttings. Ideal seeds to sow now include cauliflower, radish, mooli and lettuce.

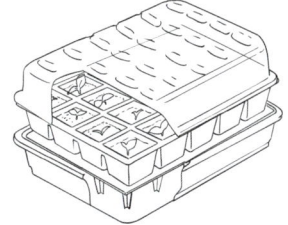

WARMER WINTERS

The British weather is changing – our winters are warmer, spring comes earlier and summer stays later. This means we can grow an increasing range of fruit from warmer climes, such as apricots, nectarines and figs.

New fruit trees are best planted during winter. Plant them as soon as you can after purchasing them in order to prevent the roots drying out, but always avoid planting when the ground is frozen. Container-grown trees can be planted any time between September and early May. If the ground is frozen or waterlogged, you can store them in a garage until the weather improves. Bare-root trees should only be planted during their dormant season, which is usually mid-November to March. If the ground is frozen or bad weather is forecast, you can 'heel' trees in the garden until the weather turns milder – you can even plant them in a pile of compost in the garage if conditions are really dire!

To 'heel' a tree, dig a shallow hole with a sloping side (dig a trench if you are heeling several trees at once) and lie the tree down so that it rests against the slope, with the roots in the hole and the canopy of the tree just above the ground. Re-fill the hole so that the roots are covered and water thoroughly. You can leave plants heeled in like this for several weeks.

A man doesn't plant a tree for himself. He plants it for posterity.

Alexander Smith

BIRDS AND BEES

FEATHERED FRIENDS

Birdfeeders are an easy way to attract more feathered visitors to your garden and they are especially welcome in the winter when food may be scarce. Aim to buy a feeder with a squirrel guard, so the contents are received by the birds as intended. Different birdseed mixes are available for feeders, bird tables and ground feeding. You can also put out kitchen scraps such as cooked rice, pasta, pastry and potatoes; along with fruit, cheese, biscuits, fat and suet, but avoid putting out spicy or salty food. (However, be aware that in putting out scraps, you might also get attention from other furry, perhaps unwanted, critters – so proceed with caution.)

Remember to leave out fresh, clean water for birds to drink and bathe in. This is important during the summer months, obviously, but it's also vital during the winter when natural water supplies may become frozen over. Replace the water regularly and rinse the container each time (dustbin lids and plant saucers work well as DIY watering holes). Keep your bird table clean and free from droppings, which can be a breeding ground for parasites and bacteria. And place your bird table or water bath away from fences or dense hedges, where predators such as cats can launch an attack. Ideally, you would want to position them with a small bush nearby, so birds can check the coast is clear before flying to the bird table to feed.

My garden is my most beautiful masterpiece.

Claude Monet

LOVELY LADYBIRDS

Keep your eyes peeled for overwintering lacewings and ladybirds. They are often found huddled in hollow twigs, tree bark or crevices in walls. You may also find them tucked away in greenhouses, sheds, garages and porches. If you see any, don't disturb them. They are great garden allies as they feed on pests such as greenfly and blackfly.

You can make a nest for ladybirds and lacewings by tying together a bundle of bamboo (or hollow cow parsley stems). Place the bundle in a large plant pot and leave the plant pot on its side in a warm, dry, sheltered spot, such as behind a shed or under a hedge. Your guests can safely shelter there until next April.

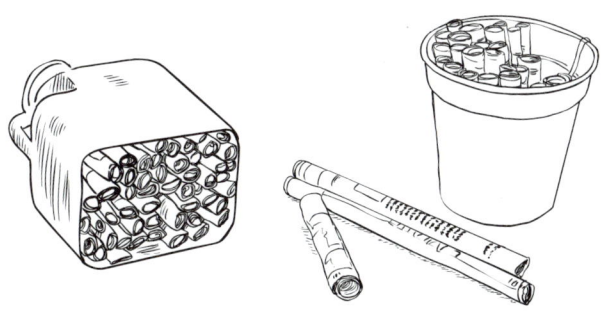

PONDS AND ROCKERIES

If your pond freezes over, toxic gases can build up which can be hazardous to wildlife. It's tempting just to smash the ice but this can injure any fish, newts or frogs that are hibernating at the bottom. The solution is to place the base of a saucepan of boiled water on the surface to melt a hole in the ice. This will allow any toxic gases to escape without disturbing the pond life. To help prevent ponds and water features from freezing in the first place, float a football or plastic water bottle on the surface. It may not look pretty, but the movement it creates will reduce the likelihood of freezing (and if it does freeze, you can remove the ball to leave a handy hole from which gases can escape!).

GARDEN LORE

Old Man Winter, or Father Winter, is the personification of the season, and has been identified with the Old English god Woden.

To dig in one's own earth, with one's own spade, does life hold anything better?

Beverley Nichols

WEATHER DAMAGE

Freezing winter temperatures can cause a lot of damage in the garden, especially to plants which have produced tender, new growth in response to intermittent warm spells. Just as we wrap up in a woolly hat, scarf and gloves, plants may also need a little bit of extra help keeping warm.

EXOTIC PLANTS

Exotic plants, such as bananas and tree ferns, have become popular in recent years. However, these plants tend to be less hardy than native species and will need protecting from the winter rain and cold. The best way to do this is to wrap the plant at the first sign of frost (usually between September and November). Choose a material which allows for a degree of air circulation. Fleece, hessian, bracken, straw and polystyrene are all good choices. Avoid using polythene and bubble wrap as this encourages dampness and rotting. A waterproof cover is essential.

GARDEN LORE

In Sussex, the ash is known as the 'Widow Maker', because large branches would often drop without prior warning. In Norse mythology, the first man, Ask, was purported to have been carved from ash.

PERILOUS PATHS!

Rainy days followed by freezing nights can turn your garden into an ice rink. Patios, paths, steps, driveways and decking can all become treacherous to walk on. Applying rock salt to these areas should help but do so sparingly to avoid contaminating nearby flower beds and hedges. A more environmentally friendly solution is to sprinkle a natural material such as sand, wood ash, sawdust, wood chips or straw over any slippery paths which get a lot of use. This won't melt the ice of course, but it will provide more 'grip' and make the path safer to walk on.

KEEPING PLANTS SNUG

Plants in pots are vulnerable to plummeting temperatures and frost, which can damage foliage and cause roots to die or rot. It's not just the plants that suffer: a hard frost can cause terracotta or ceramic pots to crack. It's a good idea to move sensitive plants to a greenhouse, so they survive the next few months, but if you don't have a greenhouse, you can wrap your pots in hessian or bubble wrap. Rolls of horticultural bubble wrap are available from garden and DIY stores but leftover pieces from packaging work just as well. Tie the bubble wrap securely in place with garden twine and keep the top of the pot open so you can continue to water the plant.

Nature's peace will flow into you as sunshine flows into trees.

John Muir

BINS AND BUTTS

WINTER COMPOST

As long as the temperature is above freezing, the composting process will continue, albeit at a far slower pace than in the heat of summer. If the temperature falls below freezing for serval days or weeks, however, microbial activity will come to a halt. Thankfully, as soon as temperatures rise again, the microorganisms will leap back into life! So continue to add kitchen scraps to the pile during winter, sandwiched between layers of dried leaves (saved from autumn) to balance the green material. You can insulate the compost pile or bin with a layer of cardboard, carpet or even an old duvet to encourage the compost to cook. If you have an open fire or wood-burning stove in your house, save the wood ash and add this to the compost pile too. Don't forget to cover your compost pile with a tarp during periods of heavy rain or snow.

NO IFS OR BUTTS

Keep an eye on the forecast and drain any water butts before bad weather strikes. In cold weather, water can freeze and expand, causing the butt to fracture (it takes a lot to freeze a large body of water however, so this may only be a risk if you experience very low temperatures over a period of several days or weeks). By March, when prolonged cold spells are rare, it should be safe to reconnect your water butt.

God almighty first planted a garden. And, indeed, it is the purest of human pleasures.

Francis Bacon

NOTES

···
···
···
···
···
···
···
···
···
···
···
···
···
···
···
···
···
···
···
···
···
···
···

....
....
....
....
....
....
....
....
....
....
....
....
....
....
....
....
....
....
....
....
....
....
....
....

....
....
....
....
....
....
....
....
....
....
....
....
....
....
....
....
....
....
....
....
....
....
....
....
....
....

....
....
....
....
....
....
....
....
....
....
....
....
....
....
....
....
....
....
....
....
....
....
....
....
....
....

FURTHER READING

BIRDS

Barnes, Simon *Birdwatching with Your Eyes Closed: An Introduction to Birdsong* (2012, Short Books)

Bewick, Thomas *Bewick's British Birds* (2010, Arcturus)

Holden, Peter; Cleeves, Tim *RSPB Handbook of British Birds* (2010, Christopher Helm)

FLOWERS

Mabey, Richard *Flora Britannica* (1996, Chatto & Windus)

Brickell, Christopher *RHS Encyclopedia of Plants and Flowers* (2010, DK)

Harrison, Lorraine *RHS Latin for Gardeners* (2012, Mitchell Beazley)

WEEDS

Mabey, Richard *Weeds: The Story of Outlaw Plants* (2012, Profile Books)

Edmonds, William *Weeds, Weeding (& Darwin): The Gardener's Guide* (2013, Frances Lincoln)

TREES AND SHRUBS

Sterry, Paul *Collins Complete Guide to British Trees* (2008, Collins)

Titchmarsh, Alan *How to Garden: Small Trees* (2012, BBC Books)

Gardiner, Jim *The Timber Press Encyclopedia of Flowering Shrubs: More Than 1500 Outstanding Garden Plants* (2012, Timber Press)

PONDS

Bridgewater, Alan *The Pond Specialist: The Essential Guide to Designing, Building, Improving and Maintaining Ponds and Water Features* (2004, New Holland Publishers Ltd)

Ponds and Water Features (RHS Practicals) (2002, Dorling Kindersley)

GREENHOUSES AND SHEDS

Hessayon, Dr D. G. *The Greenhouse Expert* (1994, Expert)

Hopkinson, Frank *The Joy of Sheds* (2012, Portico)

FRUIT AND VEGETABLES

Hessayon, Dr D. G. *The New Fruit Expert* (2015, Expert)

Hessayon, Dr D. G. *The New Vegetable and Herb Expert* (2015, Expert)

GARDEN PESTS

Hessayon, Dr D. G. *The Pest and Weed Expert* (2007, Expert)

Buczacki, Stefan and Harris, Keith *Pests, Diseases and Disorders of Garden Plants* (2014, William Collins)

ONLINE RESOURCES

www.rhs.org.uk
www.gardenersworld.com
www.garden.org
www.bbc.co.uk/gardening
www.thegardeningwebsite.co.uk
www.freshwaterhabitats.org.uk

If you're interested in finding out more about our books, find us on Facebook at **Summersdale Publishers** and follow us on Twitter at **@Summersdale**.

www.summersdale.com